June 8, 1995

Catholic Prayer Book

For my new Catholic
Husband with all
my love,

Marg

Prayer is joy
prayer is love
prayer is peace.
You cannot explain it
you must experience prayer.
It is not impossible.
God gives it for the asking.
"Ask and you shall receive."
The father knows what to give his
children
--how much more our heavenly
father knows.

--Mother Teresa

Catholic
Prayer Book

Compiled by Ruth M. Hannon

WALKER AND COMPANY
NEW YORK

Copyright © 1991 by Walker and Company
All rights reserved. No part of this book may be used or reproduced in any manner whatsoever without written permission, except in the case of reprints in the context of reviews.
Library of Congress Cataloging in Publication Data
Catholic prayer book/compiled by Ruth M. Hannon.
--1st large print ed.
p.   cm.
ISBN 0-8027-2655-0 (soft)
1. Catholic Church—Prayer books and devotions—English
I. Hannon, Ruth M.
[BX2130.C375 1991]
242'.802—dc20   90-28279
                                     CIP
Printed in the United States of America
First Large Print Edition, 1991
Walker and Company
720 Fifth Avenue
New York, New York 10019
Biblical quotations are from the *Holy Bible, Revised Standard Version*, copyright 1946, 1952, 1971, by the Division of Christian Education, National Council of the Churches of Christ in the United States of America. Used by permission.
"Prayer is joy" from *Words to Love by . . .* by Mother Teresa, copyright ©1983 by Ave Maria Press, Notre Dame, Indiana 46556. Printed by permission of the publisher.

Contents

☐ DAILY PRAYERS

3 The Sign of the Cross
4 The Lord's Prayer (*The Our Father*)
5 The Hail Mary
5 A Morning Offering
6 Morning Offering to the Sacred Heart
6 To the Guardian Angel
6 A Night Prayer from the Old Irish
7 Grace Before Meals
7 Grace After Meals
8 Act of Faith
8 Act of Hope
9 Act of Love
9 Act of Contrition
10 A Night Prayer
10 A Prayer Before Any Activity
11 The Apostles' Creed
12 Laus Tibi

□ PRAISE AND ADORATION OF THE
HOLY TRINITY

15 The Doxology (*The Glory
     Be*)
16 To God the Father
16 To the Trinity
16 The Divine Praises
18 The Sanctus
18 A Prayer to God Present
     with Us
19 The Way of the Cross
     (*The Stations of the Cross*)
23 Litany of the Sacred Heart
     of Jesus
27 Anima Christi
27 Prayer Before a Crucifix
28 The Jesus Prayer
28 O Sacrament Most Holy
29 Litany of the Holy Name
     of Jesus
33 To the Holy Spirit
34 Come, Holy Spirit (*Veni
     Creator Spiritus*)

Prayers from the Psalms

35 The Lord Is My
   Shepherd
36 Make a Joyful Noise
   to the Lord
37 A Plea for God's Help
37 A Prayer of Adoration
38 A Prayer of Thanksgiving
39 A Song of Praise
39 A Prayer of Praise
40 A Prayer for God's Help
40 An Offering of Prayer

☐ Devotions to the Blessed Mother

43 Queen of Heaven, Rejoice
   (*Regina Coeli*)
44 Short Prayers to Mary
45 Hail, Thou Star of the
   Ocean (*Ave Maris Stella*)
45 The Memorare
46 The Magnificat
48 The Angelus

49 We Fly to Your Patronage
49 Litany of Our Lady (*Litany of Loreto*)
53 Clear Star of the Morning
53 Hail, Holy Queen (*Salve Regina*)
54 An Offering to Mary of Prayers
55 The Rosary
57 A Prayer After the Rosary
58 Stabat Mater (*At the Cross*)

☐ OTHER PRAYERS

61 Prayer to St. Michael
62 Prayer to St. Joseph
62 Prayer for Our Holy Father the Pope
63 Prayer for Justice and Peace
64 Prayer of Thanksgiving
64 Prayer for Perseverance
65 Prayer for Health
65 Prayer for the Souls of the Dead
66 Prayer for Love Among God's People

66 Prayer for One Who Is Ill
67 Prayer for Protection During
     the Night
67 Prayer to the Guardian Angels
68 Prayer for Advent
68 Prayer for Lent
69 St. Patrick's Breastplate
70 Out of the Depths (*De
     Profundis*)
71 Prayer of St. Francis of Assisi

NOVENAS

72 St. Jude
86 St. Anthony
100 Infant of Prague
114 Our Lady of Fatima

Daily
Prayers

We begin our prayers, and many of our activities, with the Sign of the Cross, touching forehead, breast, and shoulders in a cross pattern. This reminds us of Christ's cross, by which he redeemed us. While making the Sign, we name the Three Persons of the Blessed Trinity.

☐ THE SIGN OF THE CROSS

In the name of the Father
 and of the Son,
  and of the Holy Spirit. Amen.

————

During the Sermon on the Mount, Jesus said to the people, "Pray, then, like this!" and he gave them the words of the Lord's Prayer.

(Mt 6:9–15). The last sentence was added at a much later date. The Lord's Prayer is one of the prayers of the Mass.

☐ THE LORD'S PRAYER
(The Our Father)

Our Father, who are in heaven,
Hallowed be thy name.
Thy kingdom come,
Thy will be done,
On earth
  as it is in heaven.
Give us this day our daily bread;
And forgive us our trespasses
  As we forgive those who trespass
  against us;
And lead us not into temptation,
  but deliver us from evil.

For the kingdom, the power, and the glory are yours, now and forever. Amen.

———

The first part of the Hail Mary is
taken from Luke 1:28 and 1:42.

☐ THE HAIL MARY

Hail Mary, full of grace!
The Lord is with thee!
Blessed art thou among women,
and blessed is the fruit of thy womb
    Jesus.
  Holy Mary, Mother of God,
pray for us sinners now,
    and at the hour of our death. Amen.

☐ A MORNING OFFERING

Dear Lord, I offer you this day
  All that I shall think or do or say,
Uniting it with what was done
  By Jesus Christ, your only Son.
Amen.

☐ MORNING OFFERING TO THE SACRED HEART

O Sacred Heart of Jesus,
I offer you all my prayers, works,
and sufferings
of this day
in reparation for my sins,
and that I may grow to love you
more and more.

☐ TO THE GUARDIAN ANGEL

O angel of God, my guardian dear,
  To whom God's love commits me
  here!
Ever this day be at my side,
  to light and guard, to rule and
  guide. Amen.

☐ A NIGHT PRAYER FROM THE OLD IRISH

May the will of God
  be done by us.

May the death of the saints
  be won by us.
May the light of the kingdom
  be begun in us.
May Jesus the Child
  be next to my bed.
May the Lamb of Mercy
  lift up my head
To welcome in the morning's light.
Amen.

☐ GRACE BEFORE MEALS

Bless us, O Lord, and these your gifts
which we are about to receive
from your bounty,
through Christ our Lord. Amen.

☐ GRACE AFTER MEALS

We give you thanks, O Lord,
for all the benefits we have received
from your bounty,
through Christ our Lord. Amen.

May the souls of the faithful
departed, through the mercy of God,
rest in peace. Amen.

☐ ACT OF FAITH

O my God,
I firmly believe all the truths
your holy Catholic Church teaches
because you have revealed them,
who can neither deceive
nor be deceived. Amen.

☐ ACT OF HOPE

O my God, relying upon
your infinite goodnesses and
promises, I hope to obtain
  pardon of my sins,
  the help of your grace,
  and life everlasting,
through the merits of Jesus Christ,
our Lord and Savior. Amen.

☐ ACT OF LOVE

O my God,
I love you above all things
with my whole heart and soul
because you are infinitely good
and worthy of all my love.
  I love my neighbor as myself
for love of you.
I forgive all who have injured me,
and I ask pardon of all
whom I have injured. Amen.

☐ ACT OF CONTRITION

O my God, I am heartily sorry
for having offended you,
and I detest all my sins
because I dread the loss of heaven
  and the pains of hell,
but most of all
because they have offended you,
my God,
who are all good
and worthy of all my love.

I firmly resolve,
with the help of your grace,
 to confess my sins,
 to do penance,
 and to amend my life. Amen.

☐ A Night Prayer

Into your hands, O Lord,
I commend my spirit.
I shall sleep in peace,
and take my rest. Amen.

☐ A Prayer Before Any Activity

Inspire our actions, O Lord,
by your grace
and continue them by your aid,
so that every prayer and work of ours
may begin with you,
and by you be happily ended. Amen.

☐ THE APOSTLES' CREED

I believe in God,
  the Father Almighty,
  Creator of heaven and earth.
And in Jesus Christ,
  his only Son, our Lord,
  who was conceived by the Holy
    Spirit,
  born of the Virgin Mary,
  suffered under Pontius Pilate,
    was crucified,
    died,
    and was buried.
He descended into hell.
The third day he rose from the dead.
He ascended into heaven.
    and sits at the right hand of God,
      the Father Almighty.
From thence he shall come to judge
  the living and the dead.
I believe in the Holy Spirit,
  the Holy Catholic Church,
  the communion of saints,
  the forgiveness of sins,
  the resurrection of the body,
  and life everlasting. Amen.

☐ Laus Tibi

Praise be to you, O Lord,
King of eternal glory!

Praise and Adoration of the Holy Trinity

Praise and adoration of the Holy Trinity should be an important part of our prayer life. We must remember that God waits to hear our prayers, to have us speak to him and to speak to us.

☐ THE DOXOLOGY
(The Glory Be)

Glory be to the Father,
and to the Son,
and to the Holy Spirit.
As it was in the beginning,
 is now, and ever will be,
 world without end. Amen.

☐ To God the Father

God be in my head
  and in my understanding.
God be in my eyes
  and in my looking.
God be in my mouth
  and in my speaking.
God be in my heart
  and in my thinking.
God be in my end
  and in my departing.

(Sarum Primer, 1527)

☐ To the Trinity

All glory while the ages run
Be to the Father and the Son
  And Holy Trinity,
    Three in One.

☐ The Divine Praises

Blessed be God.
Blessed be his Holy Name.

Blessed be Jesus Christ,
  true God and true man.
Blessed be the name of Jesus.
Blessed be his most Sacred Heart.
Blessed be his most Precious Blood.
Blessed be Jesus
  in the Most Holy Sacrament
  of the altar.
Blessed be the Holy Spirit,
  the Paraclete.
Blessed be the great Mother of God,
  Mary most holy.
Blessed be her holy
  and Immaculate Conception.
Blessed be her glorious Assumption.
Blessed be the name of Mary,
  Virgin and Mother.
Blessed be St. Joseph,
  her most chaste spouse.
Blessed be God in his angels
  and in his saints.

———

The first three lines of the Sanctus
are based on Isaiah 6:3, where the

angels are adoring God. The remainder of the prayer, taken from Matthew 21:9, was said by the people in praise of Jesus on the First Palm Sunday. This prayer is said in the Mass.

☐ THE SANCTUS

Holy, holy, holy,
Lord God of power and might.
Heaven and earth are full
  of your glory.
Hosanna in the highest,
Blessed is he
  who comes in the name of the Lord.
Hosanna in the highest.

☐ A PRAYER TO GOD PRESENT WITH US

O my God, I believe you are here
  with me.
I believe that you can see everything
I do and can know all my thoughts.

I am not worthy to be here
in your presence,
for I have often offended you.
But I know that your goodness and
  mercy make me welcome.
  May the Holy Spirit help me
and teach me to pray as I should.
Amen.

☐ THE WAY OF THE CROSS
(The Stations of the Cross)

In the Way of the Cross, we follow
Jesus from the moment of his
condemnation by Pontius Pilate,
through the carrying of the cross, his
death on Calvary, and his burial.

Since the purpose of this devotion
is to meditate on Jesus' sufferings
and death, no special prayers are
required. However, at each Station,
the following prayer may be said:

"We adore you, O Christ, and we
bless you because by your holy
Cross you have redeemed the

world." To this may be added an Our Father, a Hail Mary, a Glory Be, and a stanza from the Stabat Mater.

If it is difficult to make the Stations in a church, one's thoughts can be focused by looking at a Crucifix or the picture of the Crucifixion.

Subjects for meditation may be found in the following chapters of the Gospels:

Matthew, chapter 27
Mark, chapter 15
Luke, chapter 23
John, chapter 19

The Subjects of the Stations
First Station: Jesus Is Condemned to Death.

Second Station: Jesus Takes Up His Cross.

Third Station: Jesus Falls the First Time.

Fourth Station: Jesus Meets His Blessed Mother. (The Gospels do not tell us about this episode, but we know that Mary was at the foot of the Cross when Jesus died. We can therefore assume that she had followed her Son to Calvary.)

Fifth Station: Simon of Cyrene helps Jesus to carry his Cross.

Sixth Station: Veronica Wipes the Face of Jesus. (The Gospels do not mention Veronica, but the story has long been told of the woman who saw Jesus pass by, weak and perspiring, with his face bloody from the crown of thorns. Pitying him, she took her head veil and with it wiped Jesus' face. She was rewarded by having the Holy Face printed on her veil.)

Seventh Station: Jesus Falls a Second Time. (The Gospels do not mention this, but it is likely that

Jesus, full of pain, fell many times.)

Eighth Station: Jesus speaks to the women of Jerusalem.

Ninth Station: Jesus Falls a Third Time. (See comments about the Seventh Station.)

Tenth Station: Jesus Is Stripped of His Clothing.

Eleventh Station: Jesus is Nailed to the Cross.

Twelfth Station: Jesus Dies on the Cross.

Thirteenth Station: Jesus Is Taken Down from the Cross.

Fourteenth Station: Jesus Is Placed in the Tomb.

☐ LITANY OF THE SACRED HEART OF
  JESUS

Lord, have mercy.
Christ, have mercy.
Lord, have mercy.
Christ, hear us.
Christ, graciously hear us.
God the Father of heaven, have
  mercy on us.
    (After the following petitions, add
  "have mercy on us.")
God the Son, Redeemer of the world,
God the Holy Spirit,
Holy Trinity, one God,
Heart of Jesus, formed by the Holy
Spirit in the womb of the
Blessed Mother,
Heart of Jesus, substantially united
  to the Word of God,
Heart of Jesus, of infinite majesty,
Heart of Jesus, sacred temple of God,
Heart of Jesus, tabernacle of the
Most High,
Heart of Jesus, house of God
  and gate of heaven,

Heart of Jesus, burning furnace of
  charity,
Heart of Jesus, abode of justice and
  love,
Heart of Jesus, full of goodness and
  love,
Heart of Jesus, abyss of all virtues,
Heart of Jesus, most worthy of all
  praise,
Heart of Jesus, king and center of all
  hearts,
Heart of Jesus, in whom are all the
  treasures of wisdom and knowledge,
Heart of Jesus, in whom dwells
  the fullness of divinity,
Heart of Jesus, in whom
  the Father was well pleased,
Heart of Jesus, of whose fullness
  we have all received,
Heart of Jesus, desire
  of the everlasting hills,
Heart of Jesus, patient and most
  merciful,
Heart of Jesus, enriching all
  who invoke you,

Heart of Jesus, fountain of life and
  holiness,
Heart of Jesus, propitiation for our
  sins,
Heart of Jesus, loaded down
 with opprobrium,
Heart of Jesus, bruised for our
  offenses,
Heart of Jesus, obedient unto death,
Heart of Jesus, pierced with a lance,
Heart of Jesus, source of all
  consolation,
Heart of Jesus, our life and
  resurrection,
Heart of Jesus, our peace and
  reconciliation,
Heart of Jesus, victim for our sins,
Heart of Jesus, salvation of those
  who trust in you,
Heart of Jesus, hope of those who
  die in you,
Heart of Jesus, delight in all the
  saints,
    Lamb of God, who takes away the
    sins of the world:

Spare us, O Lord.
Lamb of God, who takes away the
sins of the world:
Graciously hear us, O Lord.
Lamb of God, who takes away the
sins of the world:
Have mercy on us.
Jesus, meek and humble of heart:
Make our hearts like yours.

Let us pray.
Almighty and eternal God, look upon
the Heart of your beloved Son
and upon the praise and satisfaction that
he offers you in the name of sinners.
And to those who implore your mercy,
in your great goodness, grant them forgiveness in the name of the same Jesus
Christ, your Son who lives and reigns
with you forever and ever. Amen.

□ Anima Christi
Soul of Christ, sanctify me.
Body of Christ, protect me.

Blood of Christ, fill me.
Water from Christ's side, purify me.
Passion of Christ, strengthen me.
O good Jesus, hear me.
Within your wounds hide me;
Never permit me to leave thee.
From the evil one defend me.
In my last hour, call me.
And bid me come to thee,
  And with your saints and angels
    praise thee,
Throughout eternity. Amen.

□ Prayer Before a Crucifix

Look down upon me,
good and gentle Jesus,
while before your face I humbly
  kneel,
and with burning soul, pray and
  beseech you
to fix deep in my heart
lively sentiments of faith, hope, and
  charity,
true contrition for my sins,

and a firm purpose of amendment.
  While I contemplate with great love
and tender pity your five wounds,
pondering over them within me,
I call to mind the words which
David, your prophet, said of you,
"They have pierced my hands and
  my feet,
they have numbered all my bones."

□ THE JESUS PRAYER

Lord Jesus Christ, Son of God,
  Have mercy on me,
    a sinner.

□ O SACRAMENT MOST HOLY

O Sacrament most holy!
  O Sacrament divine!
All praise and all thanksgiving
  Be every moment thine.

□ LITANY OF THE HOLY NAME OF JESUS

Lord, have mercy on us.
Lord, have mercy on us.
Christ, have mercy on us.
Christ, have mercy on us.
Lord, have mercy on us.
Lord, have mercy on us.
Christ, hear us.
Christ, graciously hear us.
God, the Father of heaven: *Have mercy on us.*
 (After each petition below, add "have mercy on us.")
God the Son, Redeemer of the world,
God the Holy Spirit,
Holy Trinity, one God,
Jesus, Son of the Living God,
Jesus, splendor of the Father,
Jesus, brightness of eternal light,
Jesus, King of Glory,
Jesus, Sun of Justice,
Jesus, Son of the Virgin Mary,
Jesus, most amiable,
Jesus, most admirable,

Jesus, mighty God,
Jesus, Father of the world to come,
Jesus, Angel of the great counsel,
Jesus, most powerful,
Jesus, most patient,
Jesus, most obedient,
Jesus, meek and humble of heart,
Jesus, lover of chastity,
Jesus, lover of us,
Jesus, God of Peace,
Jesus, Author of Life,
Jesus, model of virtues,
Jesus, zealous for souls,
Jesus, our God,
Jesus, our refuge,
Jesus, Father of the poor,
Jesus, treasure of the faithful,
Jesus, Good Shepherd,
Jesus, true Light,
Jesus, eternal wisdom,
Jesus, infinite goodness,
Jesus, our Way and our Life,
Jesus, joy of angels,
Jesus, King of Patriarchs,
Jesus, Master of the Apostles,

Jesus, teacher of the evangelists,
Jesus, strength of martyrs,
Jesus, light of confessors,
Jesus, purity of virgins,
Jesus, crown of all saints,
Be merciful: *spare us, O Jesus.*
Be merciful: *graciously hear us,*
  O Jesus.
From all evil, *Jesus, deliver us.*
  (After each petition, add "Jesus,
  deliver us.")
From all sin,
From your wrath,
From the snares of the devil,
From the spirit of fornication,
From everlasting death,
From neglect of your inspirations,
Through the mystery of your
Incarnation,
Through your Nativity,
Through your infancy,
Through your most divine life,
Through your labors,
Through your agony and passion,
Through your cross and dereliction,

Through your weariness and
  faintness,
Through your death and burial,
Through your Resurrection,
Through your Ascension,
Through your joys,
Through your glory,
Through the institution
  of the Blessed Sacrament,
    Lamb of God, who takes away the
    sins of the world,
    Spare us, O Jesus.
    Lamb of God, who takes away the
    sins of the world,
    Graciously hear us, O Jesus.
    Lamb of God, who takes away the
    sins of the world,
    Have mercy on us, O Jesus.
Jesus, hear us.
Jesus, graciously hear us.
We will praise you, O God,
And we will call upon your name.

      Let us pray.
O Lord Jesus Christ, who has said,
"Ask and you shall receive; seek and

you shall find, knock and it shall be
opened unto you," grant, we beg
you, that we may love you with a
whole heart, in our words and our
work, and never cease to praise your
name. Amen.

□ To the Holy Spirit

Come, O Holy Spirit,
fill the hearts of your faithful,
and kindle in them the fire of your
  love.
  Send forth your Spirit,
and they shall be created,
and you shall renew the face of the
  earth.
    Let us pray.
O God who taught the hearts of the
  faithful
by the light of the Holy Spirit,
grant that by the gifts of the same
  Spirit,
we may be always truly wise,
and ever rejoice in his consolation.
  Through Christ our Lord. Amen.

□ COME, HOLY SPIRIT
(Veni Creator Spiritus)

Come, Holy Spirit, Creator blest,
  And in our hearts take up your rest.
Come with your grace and heavenly
  aid,
To fill the hearts that you have
  made.

O Comforter, to you we cry,
  O highest gift of God most high,
O Fount of life! O Fire of love!
  O sweet anointing from above!

All Glory to the Father be,
  And to the risen Son,
The same to thee, O Paraclete,
  While endless ages run. Amen.

PRAYERS FROM THE PSALMS

☐ THE LORD IS MY SHEPHERD
(Psalm 23)

The Lord is my shepherd,
  I shall not want;
He makes me lie down
  in green pastures.
He leads me beside still waters;
  he restores my soul,
He leads me in paths of
  righteousness
  for his name's sake.

Even though I walk through the
  valley of the shadow of death,
  I fear no evil;
For thou art with me;
  thy rod and thy staff,
  they comfort me.

Thou preparest a table before me
  in the presence of my enemies;

thou anointest my head with oil,
  my cup overflows.
Surely goodness and mercy
    shall follow me
  all the days of my life;
and I shall dwell in the house of the
Lord for ever.

☐ MAKE A JOYFUL NOISE
    TO THE LORD
(Psalm 100)

Make a joyful noise to the Lord,
  all the lands!
  Serve the Lord with gladness!
  Come into his presence
    with singing!

Know that the Lord is God!
  It is he that made us,
    and we are his;
  We are his people,
    and the sheep of his pasture.

Enter his gates with thanksgiving,

and his courts with praise!
Give thanks to him,
  bless his name!

For the Lord is good;
  his steadfast love endures
    forever,
  and his faithfulness
    to all generations.

☐ A Plea for God's Help
(Psalm 38:21–22)

Do not forsake me, O Lord!
  O my God, be not far from me!
Make haste to help me,
  O Lord, my salvation!

☐ A Prayer of Adoration
(Psalm 145:1–3)

I will extol thee, my God and King,
  and bless thy name for ever and
  ever.

Every day I will bless thee,
  and praise thy name for ever and
  ever.
Great is the Lord,and greatly
  to be praised,
  and his greatness is unsearchable.

□ A Prayer of Thanksgiving
(Psalm 92:1–4)

It is good to give thanks to the Lord,
  to sing praises to thy name,
  O Most High;
  to declare thy steadfast love
  in the morning,
  and thy faithfulness by night,
  to the music of the lute and the harp,
  to the melody of the lyre.
For thou, O Lord, hast made me glad
  by thy work;
  at the works of thy hands I sing
  for joy.

☐ A Song of Praise
(Psalm 104:33–34)

I will sing to the Lord as long
  as I love;
I will sing praise to my God while
  I have being.
May my meditation be pleasing to
  him,
    for I rejoice to the Lord.

☐ A Prayer of Praise
(Psalm 63:1–4)

O God, thou art my God,
  I seek thee,
  my soul thirsts for thee;
  my flesh faints for thee;
  as in a dry and weary land
    where no water is.
So I have looked upon thee
    in the sanctuary,
  beholding thy power and glory.
Because thy steadfast love is better
    than life,

my lips will praise thee.
So I will bless thee as long as I live;
 I will lift up my hands
  and call on thy name.

☐ A Prayer for God's Help
(Psalm 102:1–2)

Hear my prayer, O Lord:
 let my cry come to thee!
Do not hide thy face from me
 in the day of my distress!
Incline thy ear to me;
 answer me speedily in the day
  when I call!

☐ An Offering of Prayer
(Psalm 19:14)

Let the words of my mouth
  and the meditation of my heart
 be acceptable in thy sight,
O Lord, my rock and my redeemer.

Devotions to the Blessed Mother

The Blessed Mother is the intercessor between us and her son, Jesus Christ. Her understanding of human frailties and strengths makes her a welcome friend in times of trouble and joy.

☐ QUEEN OF HEAVEN, REJOICE
(Regina Coeli)

Queen of heaven, rejoice!
    Alleluia.
For he whom you did merit to bear:
    Alleluia.
Has risen as he said, O Virgin Mary:
    Alleluia.
Rejoice and be glad, O Virgin Mary:
    Alleluia.
For the Lord has truly risen.

Alleluia.

Let us Pray.

O God who has given joy to the world through the resurrection of your Son our Lord Jesus Christ, grant, we beseech you, that through the intercession of the Virgin Mary, his Mother, we may obtain the joys of everlasting life through the same Christ our Lord. Amen.

☐ SHORT PRAYERS TO MARY

O Lady, make speed to befriend me,
  From the wiles of the enemy
    mightily defend me.

O Mary conceived without sin,
  Pray for us who have recourse
    to you.

Pray for us, O holy Mother of God,
  that we may be made worthy of the
    promises of Christ.

☐ HAIL, THOU STAR OF THE OCEAN
(Ave Maris Stella)

Hail, thou star of the ocean,
  Portal of the sky,
Ever-Virgin Mother
  Of the Lord most high!

Mother, as on we journey,
  Help our weak endeavor:
Till with thee and Jesus
  We rejoice forever.

Through the highest heaven,
  To the Almighty Three,
Father, Son, and Spirit,
  We'll rest for eternity.

☐ THE MEMORARE

Remember, O most gracious
  Virgin Mary,
that never was it known that
  anyone who
    fled to your protection,
    implored your help,

or sought your intercession
was left unaided.
Inspired with this confidence, I fly
to you, O Virgin of Virgins,
    my Mother.
To you I come,
    before you I stand,
    sinful and sorrowful.
    Despise not my prayers and
        petitions,
but in your mercy, hear and
    answer me.
        Amen.

After the angel announced to Mary
that she was to have a son who
would be named Jesus, she visited
her cousin, Elizabeth. There Mary
expressed her joy in the beautiful
Magnificat (Luke 1:46–55).

☐ THE MAGNIFICAT

My soul magnifies the Lord,
and my spirit rejoices in God

my Savior,
for he has regarded the low estate
  of his handmaiden.
For behold, henceforth all
  generations will call me blessed;
for he who is mighty has done great
  things for me,
and holy is his name.
And his mercy is on those who fear
  him from generation to generation.
He has shown strength with his arm,
he has scattered the proud in the
  imagination of their hearts,
he has put down the mighty from
  their thrones,
  and exalted those of low degree;
he has filled the hungry with good
    things,
and the rich he has sent empty away.
He has helped his servant Israel,
  in remembrance of his mercy,
  as he spoke to our fathers,
  to Abraham and to his posterity for
  ever.

The Angelus, a devotion to Mary, is recited in the morning, at noon, and in the evening.

☐ THE ANGELUS

The angel of the Lord declared unto Mary, and she conceived by the Holy Spirit.

(Say the Hail Mary.)

Behold the handmaid of the Lord. Be it done to me according to thy word.

(Say the Hail Mary.)

And the Word was made flesh And dwelt among us.

(Say the Hail Mary.)

Let us pray.

Pour forth, we beseech you, O Lord, your grace into our hearts, that we to whom the Incarnation of Christ your Son was made known by the message of an angel, may, by his Passion and Cross, be brought to the glory of his

Resurrection, through the same Christ our Lord. Amen.

☐ WE FLY TO YOUR PATRONAGE

We fly to your patronage, O holy Mother of God.
Despise not our petitions in our necessities, but deliver us from all dangers, O ever glorious and blessed Virgin.

☐ LITANY OF OUR LADY
(Litany of Loreto)

Lord, have mercy.
Christ, have mercy.
Lord, have mercy.
Christ, hear us.
Christ, graciously hear us.

God the Father of Heaven,
  have mercy on us.
    (After each petition below,

add "have mercy on us.")
God the Son, Redeemer of the world,
God the Holy Spirit,
Holy Trinity, one God,

Holy Mary, pray for us.
    (After each petition below,
add "pray for us.")
Holy Virgin of virgins,
Mother of Christ,
Mother of divine grace,
Mother most pure,
Mother most chaste,
Mother inviolate,
Mother undefiled,
Mother most amiable,
Mother most admirable,
Mother of good counsel,
Mother of our Creator,
Mother of our Savior,
Virgin most prudent,
Virgin most venerable,
Virgin most renowned,
Virgin most powerful,
Virgin most merciful,

Virgin most faithful,
Mirror of justice,
Seat of wisdom,
Cause of our joy,
Spiritual vessel,
Vessel of honor,
Singular vessel of devotion,
Mystical rose,
Tower of David,
Tower of ivory,
House of gold,
Ark of the covenant,
Gate of heaven,
Morning star,
Health of the sick,
Refuge of sinners,
Comforter of the afflicted,
Help of Christians,
Queen of angels,
Queen of patriarchs,
Queen of prophets,
Queen of apostles,
Queen of martyrs,
Queen of confessors,
Queen of virgins,

Queen of all saints,
Queen conceived without
  original sin,
Queen assumed into heaven,
Queen of the most holy Rosary,
Queen of peace,

> Lamb of God, who takes away the
> sins of the world,
> *Spare us, O Lord.*
> Lamb of God, who takes away the
> sins of the world,
> *Graciously hear us, O Lord.*
> Lamb of God, who takes away the
> sins of the world,
> *Have mercy on us.*

Pray for us, O holy Mother of God,
that we may be made worthy of the
promises of Christ.

  Let us pray.
Pour forth, we beseech, you, O Lord,
your grace into our hearts, that we, to
whom the Incarnation of Christ, your

Son, was made known by the message of an angel, may by his Passion and Cross, be brought to the glory of his Resurrection, Through Christ our Lord. Amen.

May the divine assistance remain always with us, and may the souls of the faithful departed, through the mercy of God, rest in peace. Amen.

☐ CLEAR STAR OF THE MORNING

Clear star of the morning
  In beauty enshrined!
O lady, make speed to the
  Help of mankind.

☐ HAIL, HOLY QUEEN
(Salve Regina)

Hail, Holy Queen, Mother of Mercy!
Hail, our life, our sweetness,
  and our hope!
To you do we cry, poor banished

children of Eve!
To you do we send up our sighs,
   mourning and weeping in this
   valley of tears!
Turn then, most gracious advocate,
   your eyes of mercy toward us,
   and after this our exile, show unto
   us the Blessed Fruit of your womb,
   Jesus!
O clement, O loving, O sweet Virgin
   Mary!
Pray for us, O holy Mother of God,
That we may be made worthy of the
promises of Christ.

☐ AN OFFERING TO MARY
   OF PRAYERS

These praises and prayers
   I lay at your feet,
O Virgin of virgins!
   O Mary most sweet!

☐ THE ROSARY

The Rosary, an ancient devotion to the Blessed Mother, consists mainly of Hail Marys, which are divided into groups of ten, called *decades*.

To say the Rosary, we begin with the Apostles' Creed, three Hail Marys, and a Glory Be. We then proceed with the decades, each of which starts with an Our Father and ends with a Glory Be.   As we pray each decade, we think about the Mystery for which it is named. The Mysteries are listed below.

The Joyful Mysteries
1. *The Annunciation* of the coming birth of Jesus made to Mary by an angel
2. *The Visitation* of Mary to her cousin Elizabeth
3. *The Nativity* of Jesus in Bethlehem
4. *The Presentation of the Child Jesus in the Temple*

5. *The Finding of the Child Jesus in the Temple*

The stories of the Joyful Mysteries can be found in Chapters 1 and 2 of Luke. These Mysteries are usually said on Mondays and Thursdays.

The Sorrowful Mysteries
1. *The Agony in the Garden*
2. *The Scourging at the Pillar*
3. *The Crowning with Thorns*
4. *The Carrying of the Cross*
5. *The Crucifixion*

The stories of the Sorrowful Mysteries are found in chapters 14 and 15 of Mark and chapter 22 of Luke. These Mysteries are usually said on Tuesdays and Fridays.

The Glorious Mysteries
1. *The Resurrection*
2. *The Ascension*
3. *The Coming of the Holy Spirit*
4. *The Assumption of Our Lady*
5. *The Coronation of Our Lady*

Accounts of the Resurrection and Ascension may be found in Mark, chapter 16, and in Acts, chapter 2. The last two Glorious Mysteries are not discussed in the New Testament. The Glorious Mysteries are usually said on Wednesdays, Saturdays, and Sundays.

☐ A Prayer After the Rosary

O God, whose only-begotten Son, by his life, death, and Resurrection, has opened to us the rewards of eternal life, grant, we beseech you, that meditating on these mysteries of the holy Rosary of the Blessed Virgin Mary, we may imitate what they contain and obtain what they promise. Through our Lord and Savior Jesus Christ. Amen.

———

The Stabat Mater is a beautiful hymn that describes the Blessed Mother's grief as she stood at the foot of the Cross. Frequently one of

its stanzas is said or sung at each
Station during the Way of the Cross.
Some of the stanzas are given below.

☐ STABAT MATER
(At the Cross)

At the Cross
Her station keeping,
Stood the Mournful Mother weeping,
Close to Jesus to the last.
   Through her heart, his sorrow
      sharing,
All his bitter anguish bearing,
Now at length the sword had passed.
   Oh, how sad and sore distressed
Was that Mother highly blest
Of the sole-begotten One!
   O dear Mother, fount of love,
Touch my spirit from above;
Make my heart with yours accord.
   Make me feel as you have felt;
Make my heart to glow and melt
With the love of Christ my Lord.

Other Prayers

The saints can act as our mediators. Special devotions to particular saints can bring us closer to God. St. Michael the Archangel is honored as the defender of the Church. In ancient times, he was invoked by those who were ill.

□ PRAYER TO ST. MICHAEL

St. Michael, Archangel, defend us
in battle.
 Be our protection against the
malice and snares of the devil.
 May God rebuke him, we humbly
pray.
 And do you, O Prince of the
heavenly host,
by the divine power,

thrust into hell Satan and
all the evil spirits
who prowl about the world,
seeking the ruin of souls. Amen.

☐ PRAYER TO ST. JOSEPH

Happy and blessed are you, O Joseph,
to whom it was given,
not only to see and to hear
what many kings desired to see
  and saw not;
to hear and heard him not;
but to clothe him
  and to guard and defend him.
  Pray for us, O blessed Joseph,
that we may be worthy
of the promises of Christ. Amen.

☐ PRAYER FOR OUR HOLY FATHER, THE POPE

O Lord God, look with mercy
upon your servant, our Pope,

whom you have chosen to be the Pastor of your people.

Grant that, by word and example, he may lead and teach those people over whom he has been set.

We pray, dear Lord, that our Holy Father, together with the people committed to his care, may attain to eternal life. Through the merits of Jesus Christ, our Lord. Amen.

□ PRAYER FOR JUSTICE AND PEACE

Almighty Father,
may your grace enkindle in us
a love for those unfortunate people
whom poverty and misery reduce
to a condition unworthy
  of human beings.
Arouse in us who call you Father
a hunger and thirst for justice,
and for fraternal charity
in deed and in truth.

Grant us, O Lord, peace in our days:

peace to souls,
peace to families,
peace to our country,
and peace to all nations. Amen.

☐ PRAYER OF THANKSGIVING

O Lord, make me thankfully
acknowledge all your many
goodnesses toward us,
  For many are the favors given
  To man while dwelling here,
  Earth is so fair that even heaven
  Could scarcely excel were you
    not there.
We thank you, Lord, for all your
gifts. Amen.

☐ PRAYER FOR PERSEVERANCE

My God, I implore you to grant me
all the graces I need to live according
to your holy law.
  Grant above all, that I may ever be
united to you by bonds of love. Amen.

☐ PRAYER FOR HEALTH

Grant, we beseech you, O Lord God, that we may enjoy sound health, both of mind and of body.

By the loving intercession of Blessed Mary ever Virgin, may we be delivered from present sorrow and attain eternal joy. Through our Lord Jesus Christ who lives and reigns with you, forever and ever. Amen.

☐ PRAYER FOR THE SOULS OF THE DEAD

O Lord, Creator and Redeemer of all the faithful, grant to the souls of your faithful departed the remission of their sins.

Eternal rest grant unto them, O Lord, and may the perpetual light shine upon them.

May they rest in peace. Amen.

☐ PRAYER FOR LOVE AMONG GOD'S PEOPLE

Loving Father, our Creator, teach us to love our brothers and sisters of every nation and race. Give us the grace to obey the words of Jesus, who said, "Love one another as I have loved you." Give us, Father, the grace to understand the sufferings of others as we understand our own. Bestow on us the gift of true brotherhood. Help us, Father, to work together to make the world a place where you will be adored by all your people in peace and joy. Amen.

☐ PRAYER FOR ONE WHO IS ILL

O God, of your mercy, hear our prayer that your servant (*name of ill person*) may soon be restored to full health. May your blessing descend upon him/her, and may it there remain. Through your Son, Jesus Christ, who lives and reigns with you forever and ever. Amen.

☐ PRAYER FOR PROTECTION DURING THE NIGHT

Visit, we beseech you, O Lord, this place, and drive from it all snares of the enemy.

May your holy angels dwell herein to keep us in peace, and may your blessing be with us always. Amen.

☐ PRAYER TO THE GUARDIAN ANGELS

O holy guardian angels, to whose care our Creator has committed us, enlighten, preserve, and govern us, and obtain for us the help we need that we may love God and serve him here on earth until we come to love and praise him in life everlasting. Amen.

☐ PRAYER FOR ADVENT

O Father in heaven, we beseech you
to raise up our hearts while we await
the coming of your only Son.

  May we, by his Nativity among us,
become reconciled to you so that
we may serve you in holiness
all the days of our lives. Amen.

☐ PRAYER FOR LENT

O Lord, who for our sake fasted
forty days and forty nights in the
desert, give us the grace to imitate
your abstinences so that we may
obtain perfect forgiveness of our sins.
Through Jesus Christ, who with the
Father and the Holy Spirit lives and
reigns, world without end. Amen.

☐ St. Patrick's Breastplate

Christ be with me,
  Christ within me,
Christ behind me,
  Christ before me,
Christ beside me,
  Christ to win me.
Christ to comfort
  and restore me.
Christ below me,
  Christ above me,
Christ in quiet,
Christ in danger,
Christ in hearts
  of all that love me.
Christ in mouth
  of friend and stranger.

———

Psalm 130 is said in services for the dead and in private prayers. It is usually called the De Profundis, the Latin for the psalm's opening words.

☐ OUT OF THE DEPTHS
(De Profundis, Psalm 130)

Out of the depths I cry to thee,
　O Lord!
　Lord, hear my voice!
Let thy ears be attentive
　to the voice of my supplications!

If thou, O Lord, shouldst mark
　iniquities,
　Lord, who could stand?
But there is forgiveness with thee,
　that thou mayest be feared.

I wait for the Lord, my soul waits,
　and in his word I hope;
my soul waits for the Lord
　more than watchmen for the
　　morning,
　more than watchmen for the
　　morning.

O Israel, hope for the Lord!
　For with the Lord there is steadfast
　love,

and with him is plenteous
  redemption.
And he will redeem Israel from all
  its iniquities.

☐ Prayer of St. Francis of Assisi

Lord, make me an instrument
  of your peace.
Where there is hatred,
  let me sow love;
where there is injury, pardon;
where there is discord, unity;
where there is doubt, faith;
where there is despair, hope;
where there is darkness, light;
where there is sadness, joy.

O Divine Master,
grant that I may not so much
seek to be consoled as to console;
to be understood as to understand;
to be loved as to love.

For it is in giving that we receive;

it is in pardoning
  that we are pardoned;
and it is in dying that we are
born to eternal life. Amen.

NOVENAS

☐ ST. JUDE NOVENA

First Day

The word *Apostle* means a
messenger.

The Apostles of the Lord Jesus
Christ were the messengers he sent
throughout the world to tell all
mankind the glad tidings, the good
news of the Gospel.

Ordinary men from the fishing
crafts of small inland seas, from the
tax collectors' benches, from the
homes of the less than middle class,
they were normally destined for
obscure lives and unhonored graves.

But they met the Savior of the

world. He spoke the compelling words, "Come, follow me." They could have ignored his invitation and returned to their nets, to their coins, to their mediocrity. Wisely they accepted his invitation. They lived for three years with the Master, received from him incredible power and authority, and went out to be his spokesmen.

Among this historic Twelve the least known was the Apostle Jude. Today, however, he is loved and honored by millions, who call him the saint of the impossible. In his honor we pray:

The Prayer of St. Jude
God, who through thy blessed Apostle Jude hast brought us into the knowledge of thy name, grant that by advancing in virtue we may set forth thy everlasting glory, and by setting forth thy glory we may advance in virtue. Through our Lord Jesus Christ, thy Son, who livest

and reignest with thee in the unity of the Holy Ghost, God, world without end. Amen.

Second Day
World conquerors we call the Apostles.

These twelve men, chosen by Christ, proved to be history's most important conquerors. Unarmed, save with the power of truth, unarmored, save for the grace of God, they moved under the leadership of Peter and of his field marshal, Paul, to win the nations for the kingdom of Christ.

They never lost sight of the Savior and of the happiness that would come to men and women who became his in utter devotion.

They spoke with his voice, repeating the things he had taught them.

They took bread and wine, and, by the same words and gestures that he had used, they turned these elements into his body and blood. "This is my body. . . . This is my blood," he had said. Then he added: "Do this for a commemoration of me."

They drove from the souls of men the worst of enemies, Satan and sin. For they exercised the power he gave them: "Whose sins you shall forgive, they are forgiven them." Everywhere they taught his way of life, the mystery of his cross, the glory of his resurrection. For he had commanded: "Go ye into the whole world, and preach the Gospel to every creature."

Among these glorious world conquerors was Jude. In his honor we say:

The Prayer of St. Jude (page 73).

Third Day
Of all the Apostles, St. Jude seems the least known.

Not once throughout the course of the Gospels is it recorded that he spoke. There is confusion about his name; sometimes he is called Jude, and sometimes Thaddeus.

In the Office of the priest the Church says of this little-known Apostle: "Thaddeus was also called Jude the son of James. He is the author of one of the Catholic epistles. He preached in Mesopotamia. Later he joined St. Simon, a fellow Apostle, in Persia, where together they brought into the faith numberless children of Jesus Christ, preaching the Gospel and spreading the faith in these vast regions and among these widespread peoples, winning them to the faith with doctrine and miracles. In the end together they made glorious the name of the Savior with their splendid martyrdom."

Since the two Apostles had worked together, their feast is kept together on October 28.

Silent as long as the Savior lived, Jude, accepting the responsibilities of his mission, travels, preaches, works miracles, writes a brief letter filled with his love for Jesus Christ, sees the faith catching fire in the souls of countless pagans, and then dies gloriously for his beloved master.

This is the great saint to whom we say:

The Prayer of St. Jude (page 73).

Fourth Day
Strangely enough, the Savior selected two Apostles of the same name. One of them was Jude, whose fuller name was Judas. The other was the infamous man, the traitor, Judas Iscariot. The name Judas has become a synonym for all that is ugly and traitorous in friendship turned to hate, trust betrayed. A Judas is a man who kisses his friend's cheek as a sign to that man's lurking, murderous enemies. So it was that Jude the saint was never given his full name, Judas, for fear that the name be a reminder of the traitor.

How different these two men in their ultimate destiny. How alike in their possibilities. Both obscure and unimportant, both are called to greatness. Each lives for three years as the intimate friend of the God-man. To each is given the secrets of the heavenly kingdom and the promise of leadership in the battle to win the world for God. Each is called a friend.

One of these two turns traitor, sears the cheek of his God with a treasonous kiss.

The other of the two, apparently of lesser talent, never—as Judas was—an official in the apostolic group, uses his opportunities, holds fast to the powers entrusted to him, loves his Savior and does his work, and ends a glorious martyr.

This is St. Jude, to whom we pray:
The Prayer of St. Jude (page 73).

Fifth Day
Sometimes we are misled by the pictures and the statues of the Apostles.

We see these men as vast in physique, with flaming eyes, hands raised compellingly, lips clearly accustomed to authority and the powerful words of the Lord.

We forget, until we come to Jude (little known and for centuries largely forgotten) that these were ordinary men like ourselves. There was little in their nature and nothing in their background to give promise of what they became. Poor sons, grubbing tradesmen, accustomed to plain fare and dull company, resigned to commonplace lives and obscure ends—there was no sign of what they could become.

Only the power of Christ made them different. Before Christ called them, the Apostles were even less than ordinary. After Christ called them and always with Christ, the Apostles were the glorious saints, martyrs, Popes, and bishops, destined to make earth ring with the greatest news since creation.

Jude without Christ. . . . a nonentity;
Jude with Christ. . . . one of the
world's truly great.

Without Christ we ourselves are
nobodies. With Christ we can do all
things in him who strengthens us.

To St. Jude, powerful with the
power of Christ, we say:

The Prayer of St. Jude (page 73).

Sixth Day
Among these ordinary men who
became the world's greatest, Jude
seems to have been marked only in
that he was more ordinary than the
rest.

We do not know whether he was
tall or short, handsome or plain.

There were a thousand others of his
name. In a crowd he would have been
lost in the routine similarity of trade
and clothes and looks and speech.

Jude had none of the qualities that
make for earthly preeminence; he
had all the generous qualities that
the Savior had sought.

From the multitude the finger of the Lord singled him out. Like the rest of men he clung naturally to his small possessions and still more to his right to fashion for himself the kind of life he cared to live.

Unlike most men he gave up all things to follow Christ, and he accepted whatever the Savior planned for him.

He could echo sincerely the triumphant words of St. Peter: "Behold, we have left all things and have followed thee." He could hear throughout his life and at the moment of his thrilling entry into heaven, "Well done, good and faithful servant." In the hope that we will follow in the footsteps of Jude, from obscurity to eternal glory, we say:

The Prayer of St. Jude (page 73).

Seventh Day
There must have been a lovely humility about St. Jude.

He left to the other Apostles the aggressive action and speech that were worth recording.

Once he breaks the silence to write a letter that is filled with his humble love for the Savior and his eagerness to see all men love him and follow him.

After a brief journey alone he joins forces with St. Simon, almost as if he distrusted himself.

Clearly he wished to share with someone else the conversions he made and the miracles he wrought and the souls he won.

After the flame and glory of martyrdom he almost disappears from history. Few altars were erected to his honor. Few churches were named for him. The fact that there had been a Judas kept people from christening their sons Jude. So few remembered to pray to this almost forgotten Apostle . . . until close to our times, this age of the common man, when the ordinary

man and woman rediscovered this
dear and humble Apostle and gave
him the compliment of their
confidence. He was a little like
themselves. They felt that a humble
saint would perhaps have fewer
clients.

To the human St. Jude, in many
ways like ourselves, we say:

The Prayer of St. Jude (page 73).

Eighth Day

So it was that in our age St. Jude
became known as the saint of the
impossible, as far as human power
is concerned. Perhaps that appeals
to our day.

Of a sudden, Catholics began to
know how great was the power of
the humble with God. At a time
when men deify fame and might,
God counters with the humble Jude.

When other intercessors seemed to
fail, they turned to St. Jude and their
petitions were answered, their needs
filled.

When the problem seemed

insoluble, prayer to St. Jude solved it.

When the difficulty was too great to bear, St. Jude somehow managed to see that it was lifted.

It was almost as if he had set the pattern for one of the branches of our armed services: "The difficult I shall take care of immediately; the impossible (in terms of human power) may take a little longer."

Faith found that humility means power in the eyes of God.

Men learned that, not outstanding deeds, but loving hearts count with the Savior; that the gratitude of Christ overflows to the ordinary man and woman who by his love and his grace attain to sanctity through the martyrdom of everyday duty.

To St. Jude, humble saint of the ordinary, we say:

The Prayer of St Jude (page 73)).

Ninth Day

We too are called to be apostles. The work of the Apostles only began with them.

That work was to be carried on by all the men and women who had learned the truth of Christ, who had experienced the joy of his love, and who wanted to share their great discovery with all other men.

Twelve men began the conquest of the world. All of us are expected to carry on that conquest.

They dreamed that every new convert would be a fellow apostle, would speak of Christ with enthusiasm, would show forth in their Christlike lives virtues that were more powerful than wordly arguments, would live the constant miracle of purity and humility and unselfish service of God's children.

The world today waits for the coming of these successors of the Apostles. Year after year young men are ordained priests and older men are consecrated bishops to do the apostolic work.

But the world needs these children of the Apostles, the lay men and women to carry Christ with them into homes and businesses, into schools and offices, to bear Christ within them wherever they go, wherever they are.

To St. Jude the Apostle we who are the sons and daughters of the Apostles say:

The Prayer of St. Jude (page 73)).

☐ St. Anthony Novena

First Day

The saints are strangely wonderful people.

And God's ways with them are a constant contradiction to the ways of human history.

There have been men who were known to every human of their generation, and a hundred years later their names were footnotes in the larger history books. Statues are built to honor the great; and before moss has formed on the pedestals, passersby wonder whom the statues represent.

Then in a certain age a man dressed in brown cloth and wearing a concealing name walks the streets of an Italian town. He dies obscurely.

Of a sudden his statue appears in a score of places. . . . in a thousand places. . . . in practically every church in Christendom. Seven hundred years later he is the dear friend of multitudes and the protector of uncounted clients. His face is known, his works are known, his name is called upon across the globe.

To the great St. Anthony we pray:

The Prayer of St. Anthony
May the festival of Blessed Anthony, thy confessor, O God, ever give joy to thy Church that her children may

be ever upheld by spiritual help and become worthy of eternal bliss. Through our Lord Jesus Christ, thy Son, who livest and reignest with thee in the unity of the Holy Ghost, God, world without end. Amen.

Second Day
Why the name, the fame, the power, and the glory of St. Anthony?

"Be ye followers of me," the Apostle Paul wrote to his disciples, "as I also am of Christ."

The blessed thirteenth century knew as its greatest son the man who most perfectly followed Jesus Christ—Francis of Assisi. He was called God's Minstrel, Mary's Troubadour, the Little Poor Man of Christ.

Gathering around him his disciples, who were patterned on the disciples of the Savior and totally dedicated to Christ, Francis formed his Little Clerks, his company of the Lesser Brethren.

A young man of Lisbon heard of these new followers of Christ, traveled the long and dangerous miles to join them, fell in love with the spirit of Francis—which was the spirit of Christ—and became St. Anthony.

No one has ever forgotten Christ. No one can forget Francis of Assisi, who brought back to the world a living image of the merciful Savior. The Catholic world cannot and will not forget the disciple Anthony, who carried about in his soul and his body the spirit and rule and virtue and perfection of his master, Francis.

To this imitator of saintly perfection we say:

The Prayer of St. Anthony (page 87).

Third Day
"Blessed," said Christ, "are the poor in spirit; for theirs is the kingdom of heaven."

To the wise of the world who lay

up to themselves treasures that fade and corrupt and melt away in stock-market crashes, these words seemed gigantically foolish.

Francis of Assisi took these words literally.

In mystic wedding he married Lady Poverty. He required of his followers a contempt for money and a love of the poor life that had characterized the poor carpenter of Nazareth.

And he came to know the truth of Christ's beatitude. The kingdom of heaven was his—God's divine life, faith, peace.

Beyond that, he knew that complete absence of care that comes with trust in God. In his hands were miracles to give to the poor and somehow, in God's sweet generosity, unfailing funds and food to bestow upon God's needy.

Because St. Anthony walked with Francis this blessed way of poverty,

today heaven is his, and a large
share of the glory and honor of earth.

He, who was poor, has enriched
the souls of millions; he, who had
no money, has become the patron
and treasurer, the unfailing banker
of the multitudes.

To the poor St. Anthony, rich in
the riches of God, we pray:
The Prayer of St. Anthony (page 87).

Fourth Day
Christ said of himself, almost
proudly, "You call me master, and
Lord; and you say well, for so I am."
He was proud to be the teacher of
the people, and he loved to be hailed
by that title.

The feet of Francis found the beautiful paths traced by Christ the
teacher. Almost avoiding the accustomed positions of oratory, Francis
talked from the steps of the
churches, from stools in the farm-
yards, from the tail of market carts,
from the slopes of Tuscany's hills.

He broke the bread of faith with the poor, the most important bread of their souls.

We speak with affection of St. Anthony's bread. Usually we mean the bread that he gave to the hungry people of Italy.

But greater and more significant was the bread of truth that he broke for the soul-hungry.

We forget that the simple Anthony was a professor of theology and founded a theological school.

We are less likely to forget the Anthony surrounded by the children to whom he told his parables of faith. We watch him as he stands amid the crowds on market Saturday, as out of his love of Christ he talks with them about the happy ways to life.

To the poor preacher of Padua we say:
The Prayer of St. Anthony (page 87).

Fifth Day
"Blessed," said the Savior, "are the clean of heart, for they shall see

God." Almost as if in fulfillment of this promise, the eyes of the great St. Francis looked up from his meditation and saw the Lord, and he bore in his body from that time the marks of the Passion. The Stigmata, they are called.

Like his saintly father, the pure Anthony, too, saw God.

The statues of Anthony retell this wonderful vision with repeated affection. For to the pure Anthony, Christ came in the purest and sweetest form, in the guise of his Infancy.

While the skeptics of his time looked upon the wonders of the universe and could not see even the footprints of God, Anthony looked into the baby eyes of God himself. Cold disbelief doubted that there was a God; Anthony held God to his heart.

He was pure in heart, and he saw God.

He saw God everywhere about him—in his wondrous works, in the beauty of nature, in the souls he served, in the upturned faces of the people who were drinking in the words he spoke, in the poor that Christ loved, upon the altar of his physical presence.

In the end he saw the Word made flesh resting in his protecting arms. As he holds the Infant Savior, we pray:

The Prayer of St. Anthony (page 87).

Sixth Day

Christ himself was poor, the companion of the poor, the benefactor of the poor.

Francis, wedded to Lady Poverty, loved and served the poor, who were her children.

Anthony, Francis's best and closest follower, could not but give his life for the poor in body and the poor in spirit.

St. Anthony's bread was before all else the truth he taught to the poor and the ignorant.

But like all wise men he knew how distracting is the rumble of a hungry stomach.

Among the poor of his time Anthony moved as father and friend.

His favorite ports of call were the hovels of the wretched; and never did this man, who had nothing for himself, come empty-handed.

He seemed to multiply the poor store of bread that he begged from the rich in order to feed the poor. Cloth in his hands did wonderful things; it seemed to expand under his touch and in the presence of the poorly clad.

It was to the poor that he came with miracles of healing. It was to the thief that he gave means of honest living. It was among the poor that he lived most happily. It was the lowly he uplifted.

To this lover of the poor, to this

servant of the poor, we pray:
> *The Prayer of St. Anthony (page 87).*

Seventh Day
St. Anthony in his day and in ours
has been known as the wonderworker.

Miracles accompanied him as did
his shadow. He dropped miracles as
he dropped his gracious and
Christlike smile.

Sometimes God gives miracles to
prove his truth. Sometimes he gives
miracles because he seems unable to
resist the needs of the saints, who
love him and have given up all things.

Never did Anthony work a miracle
for himself.

But when others had need of food
and he had no food to give them, he
asked the Lord, who had once
multiplied loaves and fishes, to
work a modest miracle for the poor
who trusted him.

And the Lord did give Anthony
what he asked.

If articles were lost, an appeal to

him located them.

Those too sick to afford a physician asked him to be their physician, and he was with the power of the divine physician.

The cupboards of the starving were suddenly filled, as if by angels' hands, with food.

And when there was need for him in two places at once . . . he was in both places, doing God's work for the poor. To this wonder-worker, who does his miracles now as he did then, we say:

The Prayer of St. Anthony (page 87).

Eighth Day

Characteristic of the communion of the saints is the aliveness of the saints.

To us who love them the saints never seem dead. For they are not dead.

We speak to them, and we know that they hear us.

We hold out expectant hands, and we bow our heads in gratitude when our hands are filled.

So it is that among all the men of history no one else seems more real and more alive today than does St. Anthony.

Thousands of churches are named in his honor. Millions of boys are dedicated to him as their name saint. Throughout the year innumerable clients find their way to his shrine and return in the certainty that St. Anthony has been listening and has won for them another of his magnificent miracles.

For the poor he finds a cure for their poverty. To the tempted he shows the sweet purity of the Infant Christ—and they are captured by its charm.

Heroic Catholic young people hear him whisper, "Come follow me, as I followed Francis, who followed Christ."

This saint of the thirteenth century belongs to the ages.

Happily we know that he belongs to us. To him we say:

The Prayer of St. Anthony (page 87).

Ninth Day

There is nothing remote and impersonal about the saints.

They are not like those men and women of importance who have no thought save for their own great interests.

By a kind of holy contradiction, the more the saints concentrate on loving God, the more they are alive to the needs of their fellowmen. The saints must see in the eyes of God his eternal concern for his children of earth.

We never think of St. Anthony as far from us.

He is so near to us that he can hear our whisper of distress when we have lost a keepsake.

Through that close union of souls he can know the secret aspirations of the young and the faint, the rising hopes that bring a sinner back from the "far country."

From the hands of the gracious wonder-worker here in our current year we take fresh and heartening miracles and receive dear and precious gifts.

The great of earth die and are forgotten. The saints of earth die . . . and lo! they live. History swallows up the men that are called powerful; heaven reveals the growing power of those whom God calls his saints.

To St. Anthony, our friend with God, we pray:

The Prayer of St. Anthony (page 87).

☐ Infant of Prague Novena

First Day

Happily familiar to Catholics the world over is the little Infant of Prague.

The dear and charming statues of him, copied from the miraculous image in the capital of harassed

Czechoslovakia, belong now to the whole of Catholicity. today they can be found almost everywhere.

Christ is a king.

This fact we celebrate in the majestic and glorious feast of Christ the King. But Christ is the king not only of power and might. He is the king not alone of terrible love, ruling from his cross, the conquering monarch entering into the glory of his heavenly kingdom.

He is also the Infant King, the king of Bethlehem and the nursery in Nazareth . . . the king too small to defend himself save by flight into Egypt . . the king small enough to hide in the Host or in a human breast. So before the little Infant of Prague we say:

The Prayer of the Infant of Prague, the Prayer of Christ the King
Almighty, everlasting God, who didst will that all things should be made new in thy beloved Son, the

universal King, mercifully grant that all kindred of the Gentiles scattered by the ravages of sin may be brought under the sweet yoke of his rule. Who livest and reignest with God the Father in the unity of the Holy Ghost, God, world without end. Amen.

Second Day

Fundamental to Christianity and basic to our faith and hope is the fact that the Son of God, the second Person of the Blessed Trinity, became a Baby.

This was the wonder that exalted the early Christians and repelled the pagan monarchs.

Suddenly the best of good news broke over the horizon. The remote God was as near as Bethlehem. The great God had become as small as a baby. The hands that fashioned the universe were infant hands. The all-creative voice that had cried the stupendous "Fiat lux" broke into the cries of babyhood.

"We can pick up our God in our arms and hold him as we hold a child." The thought made early Christians ecstatic as they took him as their guest in the Eucharist.

To the pagan world the idea was repellent.

A king must be powerful, aloof, threatening, crowned with awesome majesty.

He must be reached through messengers and surrounded by the restraining pomp of courts. So God became a Baby. Christianity was born with the birth of an Infant King. Christ's birth was like a rebirth for human souls.

Before the Infant King we say:
The Prayer of the Infant of Prague, the Prayer of Christ the King (page 101).

Third Day

It was given to Wise Men to see the kingship of Infancy.

A million million Christians have prayerfully and happily followed the

Magi as they traveled from pagandom into the very center of Christianity.

Exultantly Catholics have seen these men, the wisest of their times, pierce the thin veil of babyhood and know that a Child could be a king, and God could in his quest of hearts assume the most heartwarming disguise.

Wise as only the holy are wise, they saw the majesty in humility and the strength in love.

Before the Infant King they placed their royal treasures.

How like they were to those holy souls who in far-off Prague placed about the Infant King the trappings of royalty. The three Wise Men gave him jewels to stud into a crown, and gold to beat into fine threat for his royal raiment, and the perfumes that were burned only in the braziers that sent clouds of sacrificial incense upward to God.

History repeats itself with ecstatic insistence. The gifts that were laid at the feet of the Infant of Bethlehem, modern faith has duplicated for the Infant of Prague.

We join the Magi in saying:

The Prayer of the Infant of Prague, the Prayer of Christ the King (page 101).

Fourth Day

Our age likes to think of itself as wise and grown up and sophisticated.

Often we see our age for what it is, old and tired and faltering to an atomic grave.

It was the wisest of all teachers, Christ himself, who reminded us that unless we become as little children we shall not enter the kingdom of heaven.

Nicodemus was puzzled by the whole idea of rebirth, infancy, childhood. Christ explained to him, on that secret night of his abashed visit, the rebirth through baptism. All his life Christ explained to the tired old world of his age the importance of the virtues that keep the world young.

Sin makes men old. Virtue keeps them immortally young.

Sin speeds us to quick death. Virtue wings us to endless life.

"Suffer the little children to come unto me . . . for of such is the kingdom of God" . . . men and women of childlike faith in their Father in heaven . . men and women unwearied by the dull pounding of sin. . . .

How wise the Church to encourage us, of this weary old generation, to kneel before the holy Infant and learn once more the beauties of childhood and the virtues of a heart that never grows old.

Before the young King, the Infant God, we say:

The Prayer of the Infant of Prague, the Prayer of Christ the King (page 101).

Fifth Day
"Unless you . . . become as little children. . . ."

Who among us does not turn back to the happy days of childhood?

The incredible moment of our first communion . . . the day when in confirmation we became temples of the Holy Spirit . . . the years when mother and father were all in all to us and carried every burden and guarded us against all dangers.

Those were the days without worry or burden, without the demands of each day pressing hard upon us.

The world was new and beautiful, and God was very near. We walked with our guardian angel. We knew the saints by their favorite names.

Sin had not put its lines on our soul.

We loved purely, and we acted on warm, generous impulses.

Why regret childhood? Saints grow old; but they are the happy children of God's tenderest protecting care, whatever their weight of years or mantle of responsibility.

We might ask God to give us back the childhood of our souls, our simple faith, our untarnished love, our clear vision of the supernatural, our trust in our fellowmen, our glimpses of heaven all around us.

All this we ask of the Infant of Prague in:

> *The Prayer of the Infant of Prague, the Prayer of Christ the King (page 101).*

Sixth Day

In an age that depends upon adult cleverness, it is like God to work miracles before the statue of a little child.

The statue of the Infant of Prague has been a wonder-working statue.

In itself it is, as all statues are, stone or plaster or wood.

In its symbolism it is deep and precious and meaningful.

So it has been that near the feet of the Baby King the sick have found their health, the troubled their peace, the weary their rest, the doubting their faith, the despairing their hope.

Strangely enough, it has been toward temporal affairs, the affairs that are constantly bungled and mismanaged by the wise adults of earth, that the miracles have flowed most frequently.

Why not? God has used the wisdom of the simple to confound the wise, as he used the Babe of Bethlehem to upset the wiles of Herod and brought into ancient Egypt the eternal Word of God, his Infant Son.

Miracles there will always be, but only for the trusting hearts.

In a cynical world, only a humble heart shall be so blessed. So asking for simple faith, which is always the foundation of the greatest miracles, we say:

The Prayer of the Infant of Prague, the Prayer of Christ the King (page 101).

Seventh Day

Before the Infant Christ was born into the world, childhood was not a precious thing.

Life was cheap, and the attitude of the pagan world toward new life was contemptuous.

Only those who were strong enough to enforce their demands had any rights.

Then came the Infant Christ, and for the first time childhood became precious.

Every baby born into the world by God's hope and design was his child and heir.

Christianity saw in strong, pure, religious youth the guarantee of strong, pure, religious nations.

Marriage was founded no longer chiefly upon the lust of man and woman but upon the love of man and woman, a love that was to ripen into the living symbol of love—the newborn baby.

The child completed upon earth the Trinity of home—itself an incarnate spirit of love—as the Holy Spirit of love completed the Trinity of heaven.

As we look upon the Infant of Prague, we are glad that God became weak so that we could learn tenderness and mercy to the weak. We are glad that the Infant in the holy house gave marriage its high dignity and the home its beautiful sanctity.

Conscious of the dignity of childhood, we say:

> *The Prayer of the Infant of Prague, the Prayer of Christ the King (page 101).*

Eighth Day

Children give us an amazing opportunity to show our generosity.

The decent adult cannot fail to feel a strong impulse toward giving when he sees the smile and the outstretched hands of an infant.

Infancy becomes an excuse for human generosity.

Certainly infancy has the power to waken even in the most selfish breasts the desire to give. Christmas proves this power—Christmas that centers around the Child in the manger and the children in our homes.

Those holy souls who bedecked the Infant of Prague manifested beautifully this response of human generosity to childhood.

They clothed the Infant as we love to clothe a child in rich robes.

They placed upon his Infant head a jeweled crown.

Then they did in symbol what God had done in reality; they placed in the tiny hands of the Infant Christ the world, of which he is creator and over which he rules, and the scepter, symbol of his dominion over all mankind. So does God impress on a worldly-wise and selfish world the need of simple, generous love. And he commands our love in the guise of a baby.

Out of generous hearts we speak:
*The Prayer of the Infant of Prague, the
Prayer of Christ the King (page 101).*

Ninth Day
Christ is our king; of that there is
no doubt.

Though he was battered and
broken, he could stand in the
presence of Pilate, representative of
Rome's powerful monarch, and
accept that governor's wondering
question about his royalty.

"You say—and rightly—that I am
king."

No other king was ever more truly
king in his own right than was
Christ. As St. John points out in his
glorious opening verses, the world is
his, for he made it. When he
established the unending kingdom
of his church, he took over the
world, knowing that that Church
would see kingdoms and empires,
republics and democracies rise and
fall while it went its calm way.

But most important, he is king because a million million men and women have freely and gladly accepted him. He is the king of hearts, the monarch of souls, the ruler of men's lives, the master of their destinies. He is the sovereign who never disappoints, the emperor who walks at the side of his humblest subject.

He who said, "I will be with you all days even to the consummation of the world," has chosen to keep his promise to us in our day in the guise of an infant, if only to confound our worldliness. Before the Infant King we say:

> *The Prayer of the Infant of Prague, the Prayer of Christ the King (page 101).*

☐ Our Lady of Fatima Novena

Most holy Virgin, who hast deigned to come to Fatima, to reveal to the three little shepherds the treasures of graces hidden in the recitation of the Rosary, inspire our hearts with a sincere love of this devotion, in order that by meditating on the Mysteries of our Redemption that are recalled in it, we may gather the fruits and obtain the conversion of sinners, the conversion of Russia, and (here name the other favors you are praying for), which we ask of you in this Novena, for the greater glory of God, for your own honor, and for the good of souls. Amen.

Our Father. Hail Mary. Glory be to the Father.

Our lady of the Rosary of Fatima, pray for us!

Sweet Heart of Mary, be my salvation! The favorite Prayer of the Children of Fatima:

I. Between the Decades of the Rosary After the Glory Be to the Father:

O my Jesus! Forgive us our sins, save us from the fires of hell. Take all souls to heaven, and help especially those most in need.

II. Ejaculations
My God, I love You
  because of the graces
  which you have given
    me!
O Jesus, I love You!
Sweet Heart of Mary, be
  my salvation!

III. The Offering Before Making a Sacrifice:
O my Jesus, I offer this for the love of thee, for the conversion of sinners, for the Holy Father, and in reparation for all the wrongs done to the Immaculate Heart of Mary.

IV. Prayers of the Angel of Fatima:
My God, I believe, I adore, I hope, I love you! I ask pardon for those who do not believe, or adore, or hope, or love you. (*To be said three times*)

Most Holy Trinity, Father, Son, and Holy Spirit, I adore you profoundly! I offer you the most precious Body and Blood, Soul and Divinity of our Lord Jesus Christ, present in all the tabernacles of the world, in reparation for all the outrages committed against it; and by the infinite merits of his Sacred Heart, through the intercession of the Immaculate Heart of Mary, I pray for the conversion of poor sinners!

The editor is indebted to the
following people who have
suggested materials or who have
given assistance in other ways:
Alfred Hannon; Anthony Thomas;
Generosa Yriber.

If you have enjoyed
this book in large print
and would like to
receive information
on other books of
Catholic interest
please write to:

Mrs. Walker
720 Fifth Avenue
New York, NY 10019